Music from around the World for Recorders

MUSIC from around the WORLD for RECORDERS

Ensemble Music for
Descant, Alto and Tenor Recorders

Selected and Arranged
by
Michael Preston

Printed through support from the Waldorf Curriculum Fund

Title: *Music from around the World for Recorders*
Author: Michael Preston
Illustrator: Yukina Umezawa
Cover: Joseph Preston
Musical notation: Michael Preston
Editor: Patrice Maynard
Proofreader: Ruth Riegel

ISBN # 978-1-943582-30-3

© 2018 Waldorf Publications
351 Fairview Avenue, Suite 625
Hudson, New York 12534

Note: All attempts have been made to secure permission from copyright holders where they were locatable. We welcome contact with anyone inadvertently or unintentionally missed.

Support Waldorf Publications: Please do not photocopy from this book.

Table of Contents

Preface 7

Launching Three-Part Recorder Playing 9

Performance Notes to Teachers 11

NORTH AMERICA
Amazing Grace 16
Appalachian Hymn 18
Ashokan Farewell 20
The Waldorf Waltz 22

SOUTH AMERICA
Mi Caballo Blanco 26
Atahualpa's Farewell 28
Carnavalito 30
Peruvian Lament 32
El Condor Pasa 34
Veinte Años – Cuba 36

AFRICA
Ipharadisi 40
Nkosi Sikelel' iAfrika 42
Siyahamba 44

PORTUGAL
Pescador 48
The Fisherman – Portuguese Sea Song 50
Ballade de Saudade 52

SCOTLAND
The Skye Gathering 56
Miss Drummond of Perth 58

ENGLAND
Jack's Maggot 62
Newcastle 64
The Jolly Broom Man 66
The British Grenadiers 68

WALES
- Men of Harlech ... 72
- Shining Heart ... 74

IRELAND
- Down by the Sally Gardens ... 78
- Sí Bheag, Sí Mhór ... 80
- The Star of County Down ... 82
- Londonderry Air ... 84
- Drums and Guns ... 86

POLAND
- River Wisla ... 90

RUSSIA
- Little Birch Tree ... 94
- Troika ... 96
- Moscow Nights ... 98
- Christmas Candle ... 100

JAPAN
- Autumn Leaves ... 104
- Sakura ... 106
- Here Is Happiness ... 108

HAWAI'I
- Sanoe ... 112
- Hawai'i Aloha ... 114

SOUTH PACIFIC
- Isa Lei – Fiji ... 118
- Te No'o Nei Au – Raratonga ... 120
- Hinanui Iti – Tahiti ... 122
- Pokarekare Ana – New Zealand ... 124
- Now Is the Hour – New Zealand ... 126

Acknowledgments ... 128

Preface

An Irish scholar was traveling through Transylvania studying Hungarian gypsy violin and folklore. Caught in a storm one night, he spied a cottage light. Stumbling through wind and rain, he knocked urgently on the door. The villager threw open the door and then, with a curse, slammed it shut. So Walter Starkie took out his violin and, in the shelter of the porch, played the most mournful air he knew. The door burst open again. This time, the villager rushed out, joyfully embraced the professor like a long-lost relative, and dragged him in to eat with his family and take shelter from the storm overnight.*

When I lived in Hawai'i, I was once visiting the Polynesian Cultural Center, north of Honolulu, where many cultures from the Pacific display crafts, dance and music. In the Fijian area, a man and woman were sitting inside the *valé*, waiting to entertain tourists with their craft work. Next to them was a ukulele. I asked if I could play it and they assented. I began to sing "Isa Lei," a well-known and lovely song from Fiji. I had only sung a few bars into the piece, when they jumped up and shook my hands with great joy. I realized then how much it meant to them that someone from another culture should know and sing the words of one of their national songs. Music communicates powerfully and immediately!

My own childhood, with a musical, Irish father, began in Africa and then New Zealand. After high school, I was a volunteer for a year in an island of Vanuatu, near Fiji. Those formative years planted in me a deep respect and love for folk music from around the world.

The idea to assemble pieces into a book arose in journeying through the grades as a Waldorf class teacher. Students in the different classes that I taught were natural, open-hearted travelers, ready to enter the worlds of the places they studied, through art, craft, singing, movement, and sometimes dancing. They also had another doorway to new lands and cultures—through playing together on their recorders.

Most Waldorf students learn flute playing in the first two to three grades on a pentatonic pipe. This is taught by ear, until perhaps the second semester of the third grade. Teachers are encouraged in their training that, along with singing, it is very beneficial to play a little music, every day, in their morning lessons. This leads to fine

---

Raggle Taggle: Adventures with a Fiddle in Hungary and Romania (London: John Murray, 1940)

ear training, and, as with children in many rural cultures or where live music is still vital, music becomes second nature to the children, like learning another language by being immersed in it. We also now know, through two decades of neuroscience, that the use of our hands acts as aerobic stimulation and fires new growth for the brain. Nimble exercise of the fingers on pipes or recorders, especially daily, is a powerful developmental ally![1]

For the middle school years, there are added benefits of ensemble recorder playing, where self-consciousness in singing particularly impacts the boys whose voices are changing. A recorder allows a teenager to invest in musical feeling without shyness. Three-part ensemble playing also has a vital and health-giving power, blowing a daily breeze of social harmony into a class.

With fine insight, Rudolf Steiner pointed out that teen years are often experienced as "a gentle rain of pain." Choral music-making, vocal or instrumental, helps the sun break through the clouds, bringing peace and reassurance to the heart as an innate member of a greater soul of the world.

Recognizing the value of daily music-making in my classes, and through a love of music from around the world, I started to bring together pieces from a variety of sources, with the aim of making them visually easy to see, not hard to sight-read, yet varied and interesting with the possibility of harmonic accompaniment. From the fifth grade onward, I began to collect songs and instrumental pieces that I liked and, with the aid of a music program, arranged them in folders for students to play.

World music sources were tapes and compact discs, international folk song books, dance tunes from periods playing in contra-dance groups, Pacific music I was exposed to in Hawai'i—anything I heard that became a delightful new friend met in a different land.

The forty-four arrangements in this renewed collection[2] honor the wealth and variety of many different cultures' musical expressions. They are dedicated in grateful friendship to the minds and hearts of people in other lands. May those who play these songs find among them lifelong friends and treasures and give thanks to the creator for such a varied and beautiful world!

– Michael Preston
September 2017

---

[1] "Learning Arts and the Brain," DANA Foundation, 2007.
[2] *Music from around the World for Recorders*, first edition (Chatham, NY: Waldorf Publications, 2001)

Launching Three-Part Recorder Playing

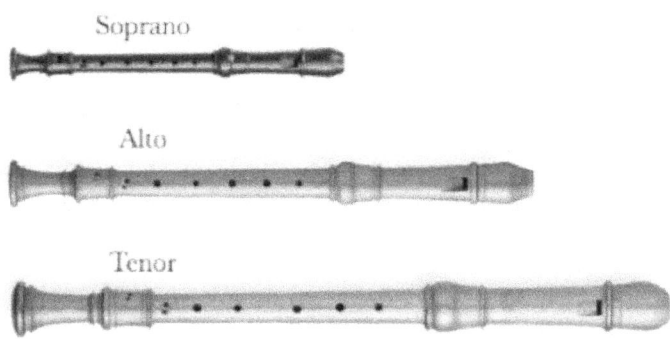

Most Waldorf teachers will have become familiar with teaching and playing the Soprano or descant recorder up to 6th grade. Stepping up to three-part playing can seem a big hurdle the first time a teacher contemplates taking this on. However, be assured, this is really not as difficult as it seems!

LAUNCHING TENORS: The fingering and sight-reading on the Tenor is exactly the same as for the Soprano recorder. It is just that the instrument is bigger and the tone deeper, and for many students it is a stretch for the fingers of the right (lower) hand. If you have two or three Tenors available for your class, make sure the students who want to play one can reach the lower notes! If they can, then that is all that is needed short of sight-reading their part.

LAUNCHING ALTOS: The Alto recorder, which is a lovely size for middle school students and has a warm, friendly tone, is the teacher's main challenge. All the holes are stopped with the same fingers so, in that regard, the Alto is an easy transition to a more relaxed size.

The challenge is the change of key. When you stop all the holes on the Soprano and Tenor, you will be playing a C. However, when you do the same with the Alto you are not playing a C, but an F.

Moving up the scale on an Alto: A Soprano D fingering on the Alto will sound as a G; E will sound as an A; F as a B; G as a C; and so on.

There are simple books that can lead students to learn to sight-read the Alto notes, so in the summer before, or early in the 6th grade, you need to find and choose one. A fine recorder approach that builds on existing skills with the Soprano (descant) recorder and transfers those skills to Alto (treble) recorder is: *From Descant to Treble* by Brian Bonsor (Schott, 1985). If, as occasionally happens, a teacher wants the whole class to learn Alto, then *Do It! Learn Alto Recorder* by James Froseth may be more suitable.

Armed with a simple step-by-step book, I can achieve classroom Alto "literacy" without altering the day-to-day flow of class music-making and without adding noticeably to my own workload.

After sorting the class (where possible, best by student choice) into the three sections, making sure the balance of lower instruments to Sopranos was good, I then arranged two lunch-hour sessions per week (approximately 15 minutes each). Using the sequence of the book, in about three weeks or fewer, I had taught the basics of Alto sight-reading.

Then I made sure that the first couple of three-part pieces for the whole class were especially easy for the Altos. In this relatively stress-free way, we were launched. Through regular playing, the Altos were perfectly secure by the end of the first semester. In addition, there is almost always a leader who emerges in the Alto group who is able to help his or her classmates with finding the fingering for a new note.

By the time you reach 8th grade, with regular playing each week, your class, as a group, will be able to play most music in easy keys straight off as an ensemble!

Performance Notes for Teachers

The songs in this book are all arranged to be on two facing pages, and all are in simple keys and related minors. The accompanying chords are also easy to play.

COUNTING IN

Many tunes begin with one or more pick-up beats in the first measure. Pick-up beats are simply beats that sit at the beginning of a tune but do not start on the first (down) beat. For example, in a four beat measure, a piece could launch the melody on the 2nd, or 3rd or, more often, on the 4th beat.

For example, in the US folk song, "O Susanna," the tune starts "Oh I come from Alabama..." In this case, the first two 8th notes— **"Oh I"—are in the pick-up measure**, then *"come"* is the first note and downbeat of the next full measure. So you would count it like this:

One **full** measure to set the tempo: one, two, three, four. And then the pick-up measure: one, two, three (and you come in on the 4th beat), "Oh I." Then "come" is the first downbeat of the following (second) measure.

Once you are launched this way, everything will fall into place rhythmically. Set the beat (conducting, tapping, strumming, etc.) with your class by always giving a whole measure (for nothing) followed by counting in the missing beats of the pick-up measure to lead in to the tune. You will hear the "count in" on the guitar on every track of the CD.*

Note: Not every tune has a pick-up bar or measure; many start on the first downbeat, so then you would count out one bar (for nothing) and start playing on the first beat of the first measure.

---

* CDs can be obtained by contacting publications@waldorf-research.org

SOPRANO-MELODY LINE

In some places there are two notes given for certain notes. These offer performance options. In the Soprano part, you will sometimes see a note lower than middle C (the lowest scored note for the descant recorder). This is because the melody actually drops to this note (for example, in "Ashokan Farewell"). In such cases, the addition of a violin, which most Waldorf classes are likely to have, is very helpful to be able to play notes below middle C and add its own special timbre.

ALTO

In the Alto part, a note higher than the high C may be too hard for most students to reach, so a lower alternative is given.

TENOR

Creating harmony in the Alto and Tenor lines is a balance between the ideal phrase and playability. Where possible, I have taken into account that the lowest notes, particularly C and C#, are often hard to sound successfully on the Tenor recorder, as well as being a stretch for the right hand! Where musically possible, I have moved some phrases up to avoid this challenge.

BASS

I have not added a bass part except in a few pieces. However, every song has chords. If your school or class has some deep chime bars, a student can strike the chime bar sharing the chord's name (found above the top, Soprano line) on the first downbeat or whenever the chord changes. This works even if the chord is a minor or a 7th.

If one of your students plays bass or even cello in the string orchestra, the same approach can be used. It greatly enhances the sound and can often give a student who has recently joined the class and cannot play recorder yet something very valuable to add.

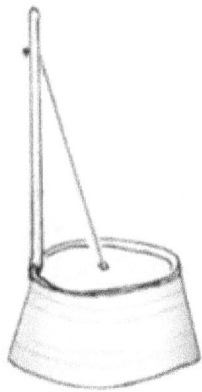

OTHER INSTRUMENTS

Using the talents of the students to add instruments such as flute, violin and rhythm (shakers, tambourine, etc.), according to the character of the piece of music, is highly recommended! You can hear some examples in certain tracks on the CD.* Two of the African pieces really lend themselves to rhythm. Use your musical judgment and experiment! You can add a washtub bass (aluminum tub from the hardware store with a broom handle and thin rope to a hole drilled in the middle). A wooden tea chest works even better.

---

* CDs can be obtained by contacting publications@waldorf-research.org

OVERALL BALANCE

Remember, the final sound balance in your class is important. The Soprano recorder is very dominant (actually sounding an octave higher than it is written in the treble clef), so you will need to have up to **at least** half of the class on Alto and Tenor to balance the Sopranos! If you have a mix, such as a violin or side-flute on the main melody (soprano line), that will add to the strength and richness of the overall sound.

As the teacher, if you can play a few chords on guitar, you will have the fun of playing along with the class and adding rhythm and harmonic richness to the music.

ORNAMENTING THE MELODY LINE

Many folk tunes lend themselves to ornaments such as trills or turns. The lead player on the demo CD,* on my suggestion, freely ornamented melodies (Irish music really calls for this!) so you can hear the mood of the tune better. I have not found many students who can trill, but you could look for a little lesson online for yourself, and then teach one or two talented Soprano players how to ornament melodies that call for it.

ENSEMBLE LAYERING

Once all sections of the class can play their parts, there are many tunes in this book that will sound all the better if you experiment with letting some players (for example a trio of Soprano, Alto and Tenor) "solo" the opening of the tune up to a certain bar (I have suggested this in the notes to some tunes), and then have the rest of the class join in.

If you have a good violinist or flautist, many tunes will sound lovely with a solo verse or passage. Some students really enjoy being able to extend their orchestral skills into the classroom in this way!

EXPERIMENT!

Finally, experiment and have fun! The discovery of the addition of a different instrument (a student once used a rain stick to make the sound of the sea washing up on the beach to introduce and end one of our sea songs) can be a joyful experience and fun in an assembly! The CD* that accompanies this book will give you a sense of the piece, and possibly extra ideas for how it can be enhanced in performance.

---

* CDs can be obtained by contacting publications@waldorf-research.org

North America

Amazing Grace – Southern Harmony

The words were written by John Newton; it is believed, however, that the tune predated him. It was popularized in the Civil Rights movement of the 1960s. It is said to be the most popular and iconic United States hymn, and there are literally hundreds of arrangements and recordings. This version is based on an early Southern harmony.

Appalachian Hymn – Traditional

The melody of this hymn, also a traditional Southern harmony, has a plaintive, Celtic lilt. It lends itself to an opening solo on the first section, especially a violin, but I think it could be very effective with a mandolin or chime bar opening.

Ashokan Farewell – Jay Ungar

This beautiful and haunting tune, composed by Jay Ungar and used in Ken Burns's Civil War series on PBS, is a fine song for the U.S. history block in 8th grade. A violin solo can be a beautiful way to begin this piece. Many thanks to Jay Ungar and Swinging Door Music for his kind permission to include this arrangement!

The Waldorf Waltz – Jim Fownes

This charming and sinuous waltz was composed in honor of the Honolulu Waldorf School for allowing a contra-dance group called The Cast-Offs to hold a dance once a month in its hall. Jim Fownes, the composer, added a second part at my request, and I later added the Tenor part. Many thanks to Jim for his generosity in freely allowing this composition to be included.

Amazing Grace

John Newton

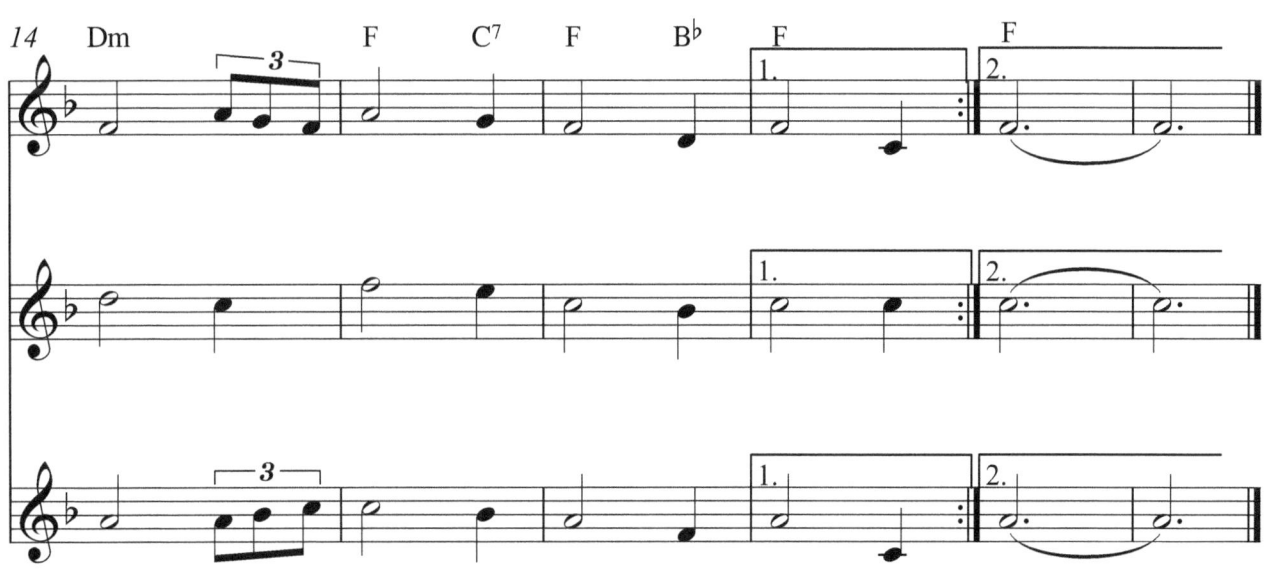

Appalachian Hymn

Moderato ♩ = 105

Traditional

Play mp for final time

Ashokan Farewell

Jay Ungar

©1983 by Swinging Door Music-BMI
Arranged by kind permission

The Waldorf Waltz

By kind permission of Jim Fownes 2017

South America

Mi Caballo Blanco – Chile – Francisco Flores del Campo

This is a beautiful song about a white horse who is our closest friend and whose spirit will accompany us even to death. This song is very suitable for fifth grade onward. A tambourine or maracas really adds to this piece.

Atahualpa's Farewell – M. Preston

I have always felt a great sadness about what happened to the Inca Emperor, Atahualpa. Yet the Inca Empire had a glorious, almost victorious, quality that seems to live on in much of Peruvian music. This tune holds energy, melancholy and perhaps a sense of victory in it. If you have rhythm instruments and a strumming instrument, you can really bring this alive. A *charango* or ukulele can be used to great effect.

Carnavalito – Argentina – Traditional

This song has a typical short-long, short-long-long rhythm of many Andean dance tunes. It has up-beat energy and vitality, and again, rhythm instruments add to its mood.

Peruvian Lament – Traditional

The original to this piece goes under another name, but I have not been able to find it. This is my own title. It has a wistful and melancholy quality. Chime bars arranged in chords work very well with this. The Andean bass drum, called a *bombo*, or a similar soft deep sound, can also be very effective in this piece, to give a steady, processional beat to the tune.

El Condor Pasa – Peru – Traditional

Probably the best known tune from Peru, this was popularized by Paul Simon in the 1960s. It is claimed by some that the variation on the second page of this score is not an original part of this melody. I have included it as I have heard it played that way by several groups, and it seems to belong with the arc of the piece.

Veinte Años – Cuba – Carlos Puebla

Cuba is not considered part of South America, but as there is no Central American or Caribbean section in this book, I have included the tune here. It was popularized when Ry Cooder founded the Buena Vista Social Club, a group of aging, wonderful Cuban musicians, completely unselfconscious in their masterful rhythm and unity of performance. This is a gem of a piece, both in harmony and rhythm. It is very suitable for the eighth grade. Warmest thanks to EGREM Music and Raul Pileta for original permission to include this arrangement, and to Carlos Puebla, one of Cuba's finest composers!

South America

Mi Caballo Blanco

Atahualpa's Farewell

Brightly and rhythmically ♩ = 120 **M. Preston 2004**

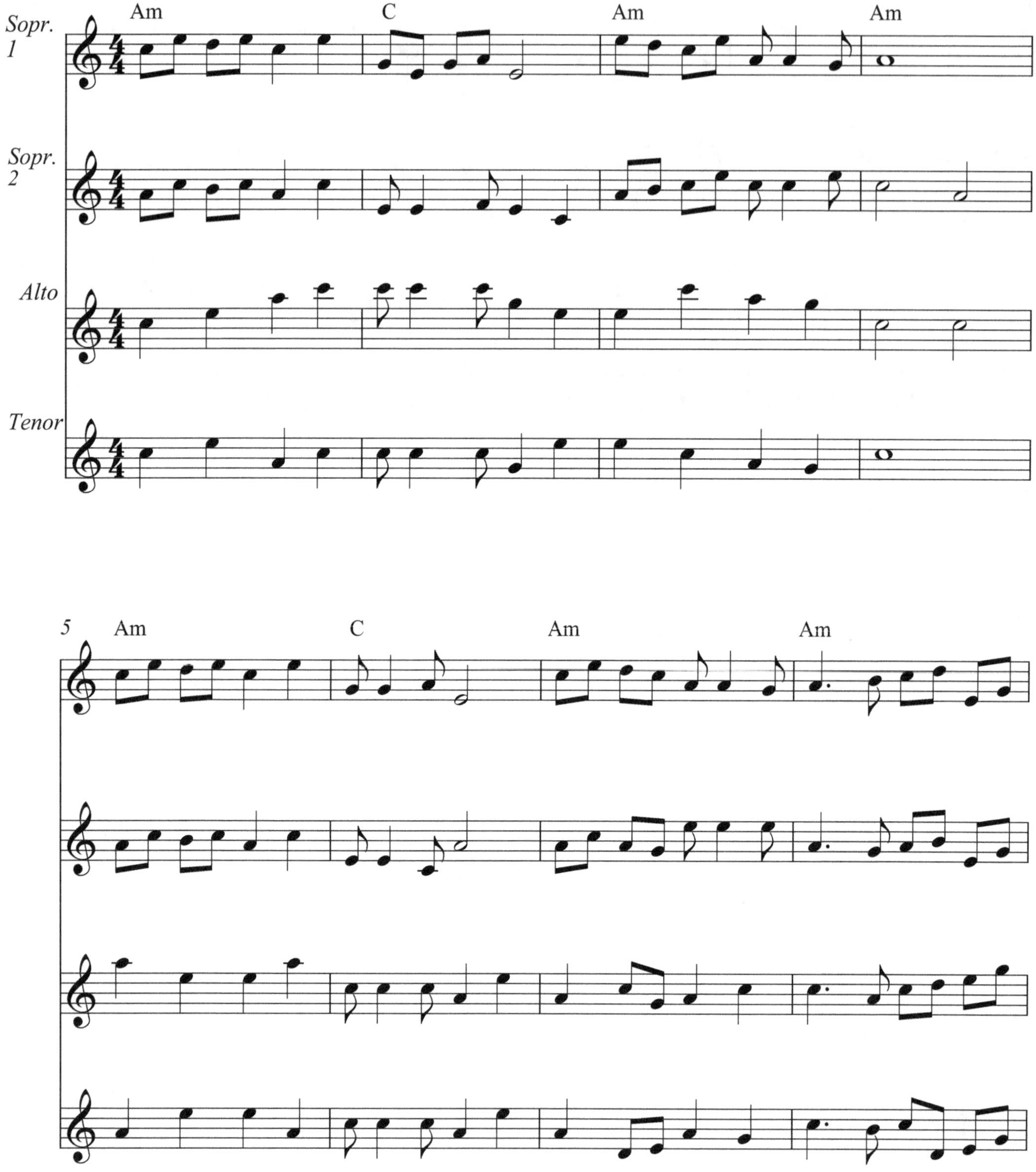

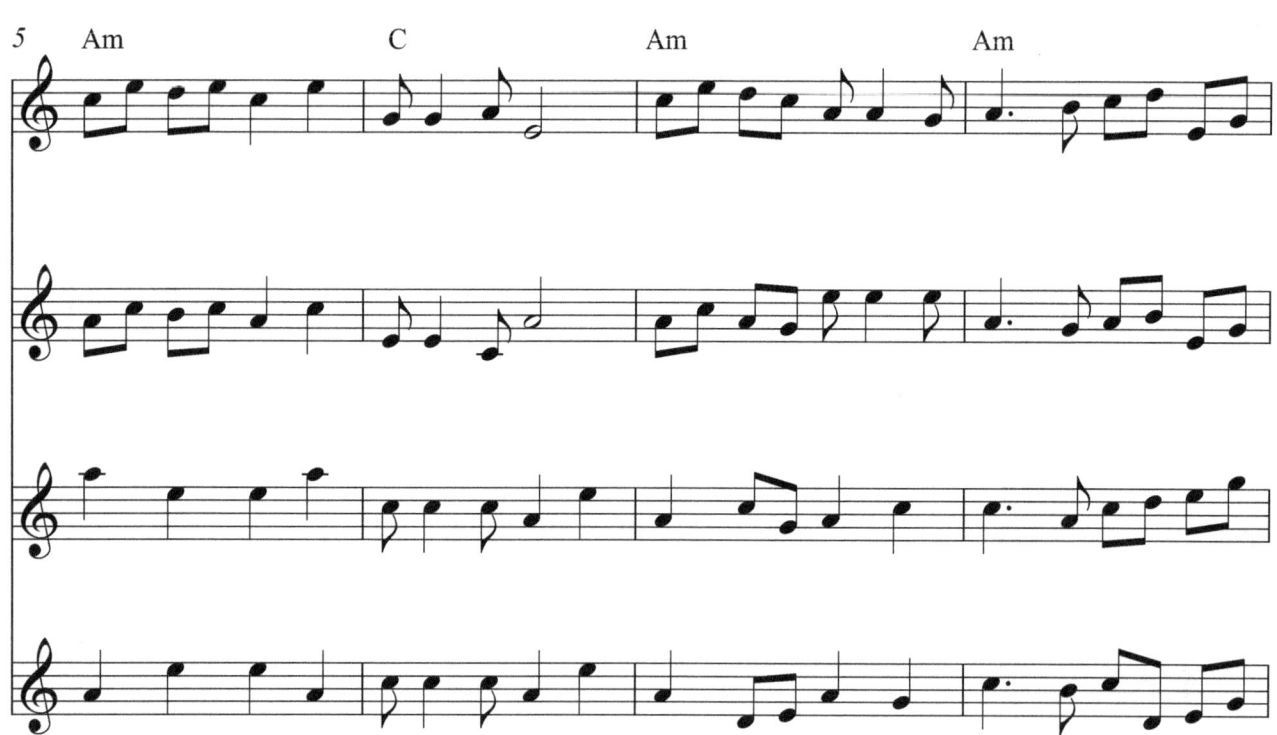

Carnavalito

Andantino ♩ = 70

Traditional Argentina

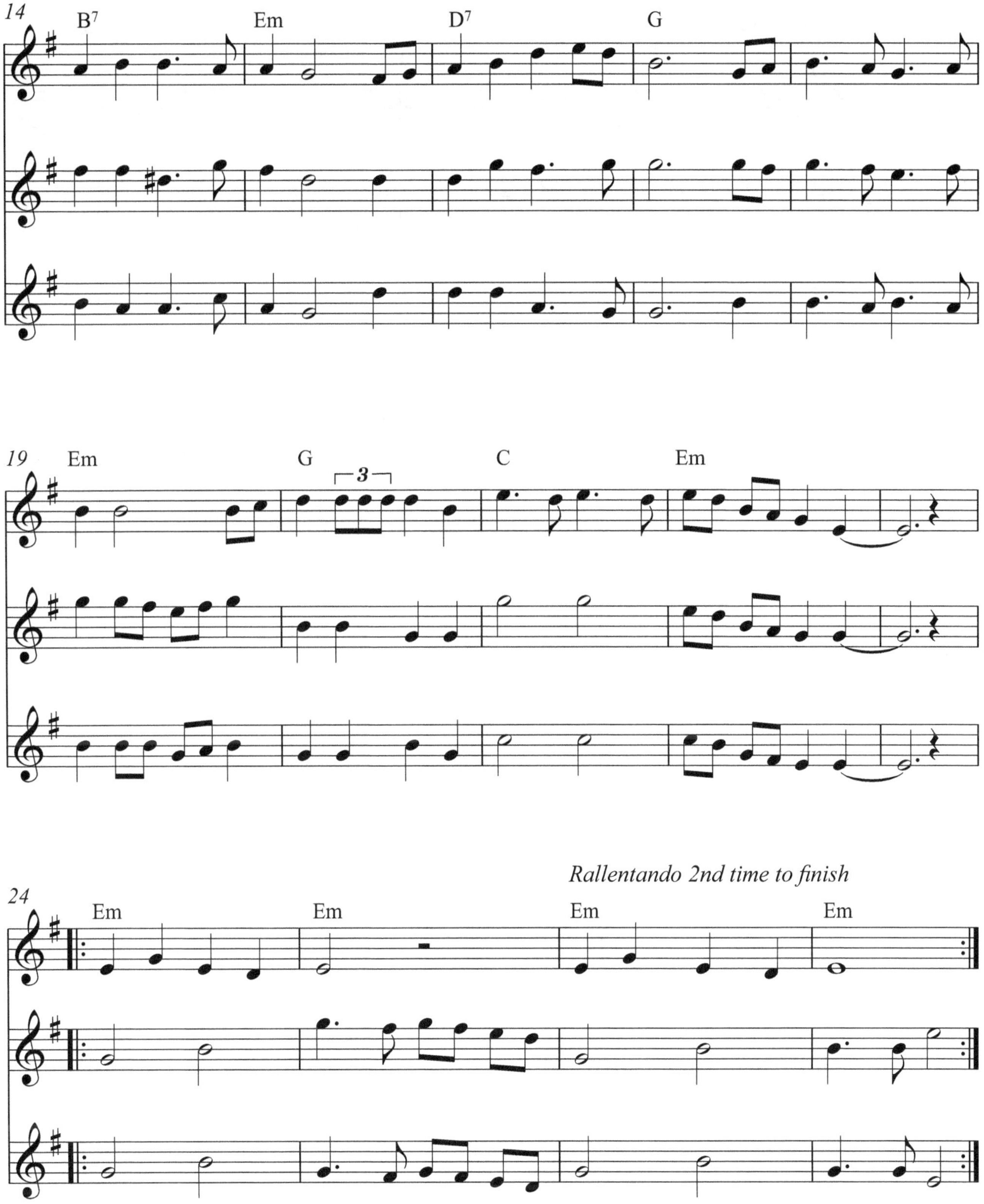
14
B7
Em
D7
G
19
Em
G
3
C
Em
Rallentando 2nd time to finish
24
Em
Em
Em
Em

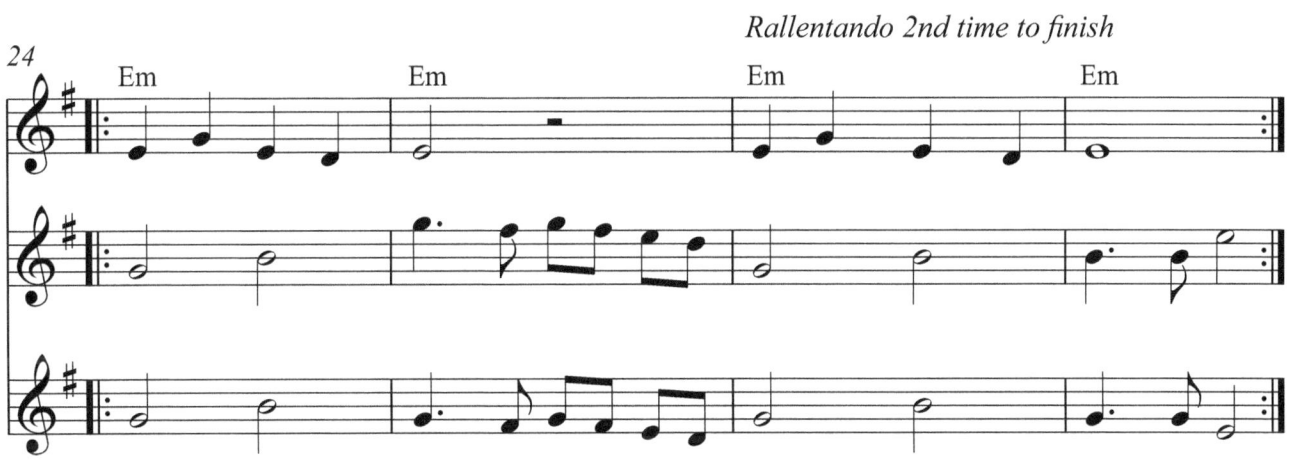

El Condor Pasa

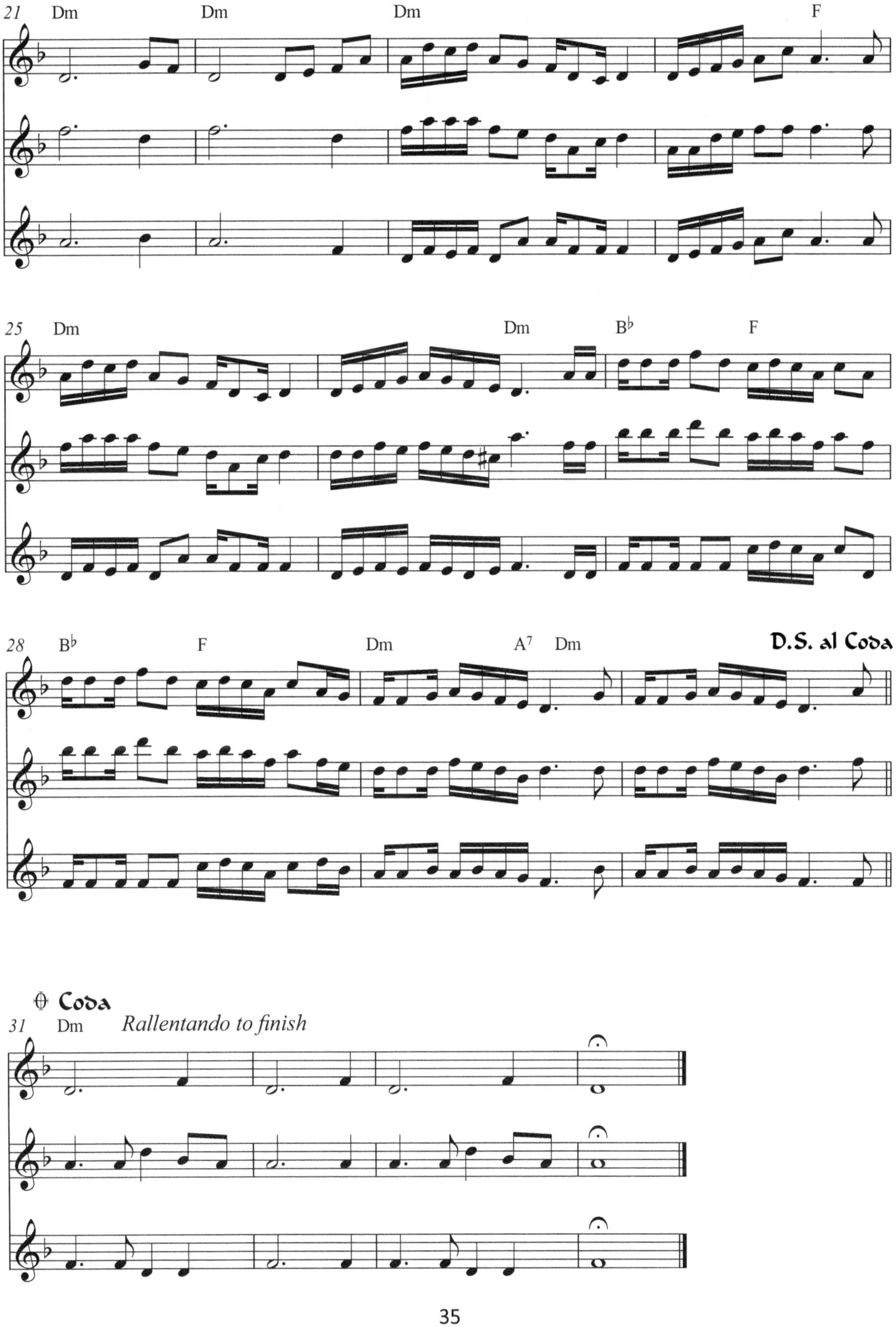
21
Dm
Dm
Dm
F
25
Dm
Dm
B♭
F
28
B♭
F
Dm
A7
Dm
D.S. al Coda
Coda
31
Dm
Rallentando to finish

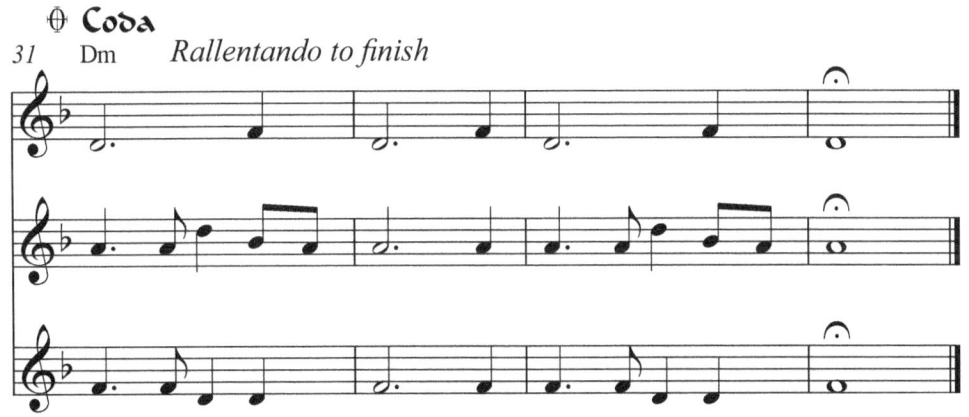

Africa

Ipharadisi – Traditional

This piece is full of lively, upbeat rhythm. To add interest I have modulated the tune with a bridge passage from the key of G up to C and back. It definitely needs, and is enriched by, rhythm instruments as backing!

Nkosi Sikelel' iAfrika – Traditional

This beautiful South African anthem can be heard most movingly in the film *Cry Freedom* about the anti-apartheid movement in pre-independent South Africa. It was sung by a huge crowd at Steve Biko's funeral. It should be played slowly and with deep feeling.

Siyahamba – South Africa – A. Nyberg (ed.)

An inspiring South African hymn, "We Are Marching in the Light of God" is exciting musically for its triplet rhythms and harmony, all with typically African joy! It is wonderful to sing. If you sing it, then recorders can be blended in, or act as an instrumental ritornello between verses. You can find the words in some hymn books or purchase the sheet music from Walton Publishers. Many thanks to them for permission to arrange this piece and include it here.

Africa

Ipharadisi

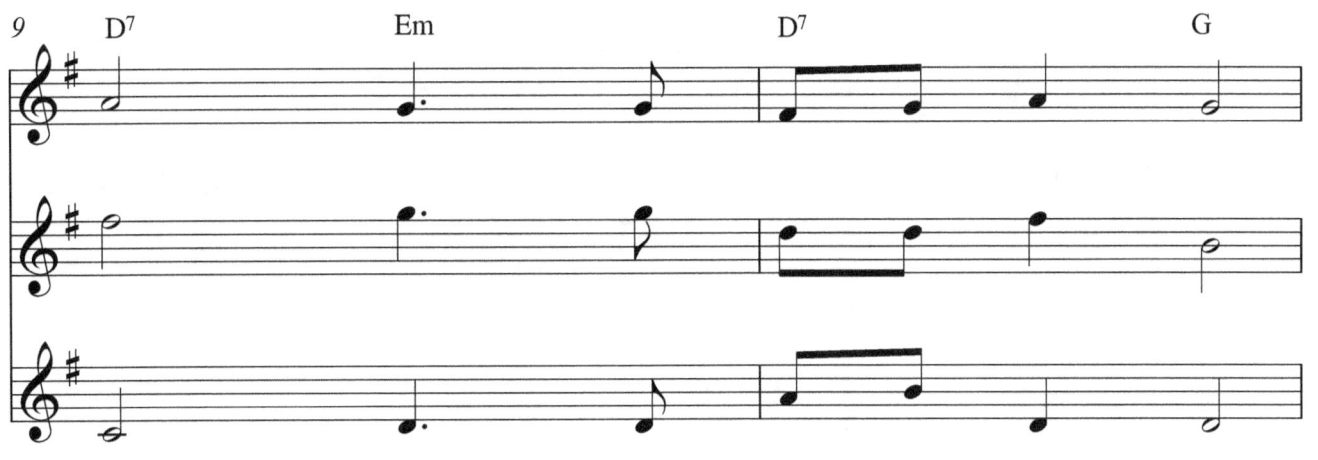

Siyahamba
We Are Marching in the Light of God

A. Nyberg (ed.)

©1984 Utryck AB, admin. Waldorf Music Corp., a Division of GIA Publications, Inc.
All rights reserved. Used by permission.

Portugal

Pescador – Traditional

This simple song about a fisherman has the typical minor to major and back to minor quality of much Portuguese music. It is in common time, in contrast to the next song, also about a fisherman!

The Fisherman – Portuguese Sea Song – Florence Hudson Botsford

Set in rolling 6/8 rhythm, this piece has the passion of the Portuguese soul in it and is very well arranged. You can use it when studying the great explorers in seventh grade. I have simply added the Tenor part. A chordal accompaniment on guitar or chimes works very well in one-two-and-three and one-two-and-three-and rhythms. Many thanks to Schirmer Publications for allowing us to use this piece.

Ballade de Saudade – Traditional Fado

The *Fado* or "song of fate" is a very important part of Portuguese music. The ringing tones of the Portuguese *guitarra*, along with a regular guitar, called *viola*, in Portuguese, usually accompany a powerful female singer. Some Fados like this one, are instrumental pieces. *Saudade* means "longing" but also "passionate feeling."

Pescador

Moderato - peacefully ♩ = 100

Portuguese Traditional

The Fisherman
Portuguese Sea Song

Flowing ♩. = 50

Florence Hudson Botsford

50

THE FISHERMAN from the Botsford Collection of Folk Songs
by Florence Hudson Botsford
Copyright © 1931 (Renewed) by G. Schirmer, Inc. (ASCAP)
International copyright secured. All rights reserved.
Reprinted by permission.

Ballade de Saudade

Portuguese Fado

Scotland

The Skye Gathering – Traditional

In this tune you will find what is called the "Scotch snap," quite unique to Scottish music. It is often used in Strathspey dances. Instead of the paired, long-short eighth notes often found in Irish dance music, you have here the reverse; sometimes two short-long pairs of eighth notes. This gives a bracing quality that is quite distinctive in much Scottish music. Thanks to the folklorist, Tim Porter, who gave me this tune.

Miss Drummond of Perth

This is a much loved Scottish Strathspey. I have modulated it from the key of D minor on the first page to E minor on the second page, with a bridge back to finish on the first page. The second page keeps the melody but gives the Altos and Tenors a rest, by playing slower, drone-like notes, before returning to the vigor of the first page.

Scotland

The Skye Gathering

England

Jack's Maggot – Playford Dance – Traditional

This tune dates back to 1716. A "maggot" is a light-hearted, whimsical tune. This one is a well-known and popular Morris Dance tune with lots of earthy zest, typical of English country dance music. Morris Dancing is very ancient and still practiced all over England. There are many groups in the United States, too. Thanks to Tim Porter from the Cotswolds, near Oxford, for his original two-part arrangement.

Newcastle – Playford

This is also a very well-known Morris tune, often played for Maypole dances. In spite of the robust rhythms, many English tunes have memorable and often sweet melodies. This is definitely one of those!

The Jolly Broom Man – Traditional

Another Morris Dance tune, I have put this into two keys for variation and interest. It is a great tune for May Day. I was given this tune by a very avid and kind Morris Dancer from Santa Cruz, California!

These three pieces, in different keys, could be played as a set for May Day, perhaps when the classes are settling in before the dancing begins.

The British Grenadiers – Traditional March

This tune dates from the 17th century. Some sources claim it was originally a Playford tune, others that the melody came from Holland. Since 1716, it has been a military tune. I have included it here as it is a very well-known English marching piece and might be a good tune to use for the "Redcoats" in 8th grade history of the American Revolutionary War.

England

Jack's Maggot

Trad. Playford Dance

Original, two-part arrangement by Tim Porter, Green Branch Theater Band
Moreton-in-the-Marsh, Glouchestershire, 1978

Newcastle

Allegretto ♩=130

Playford Morris Tune

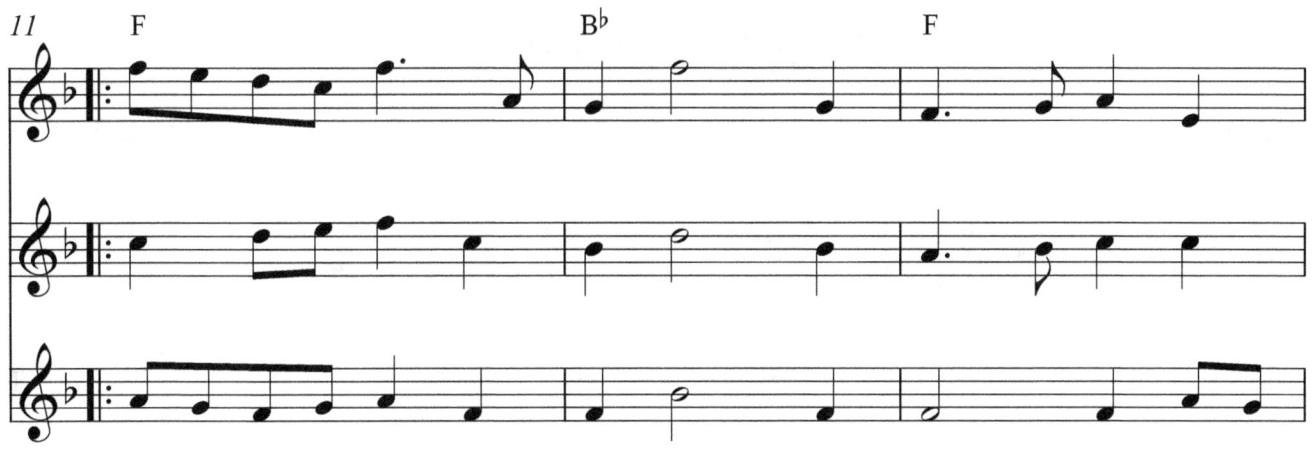
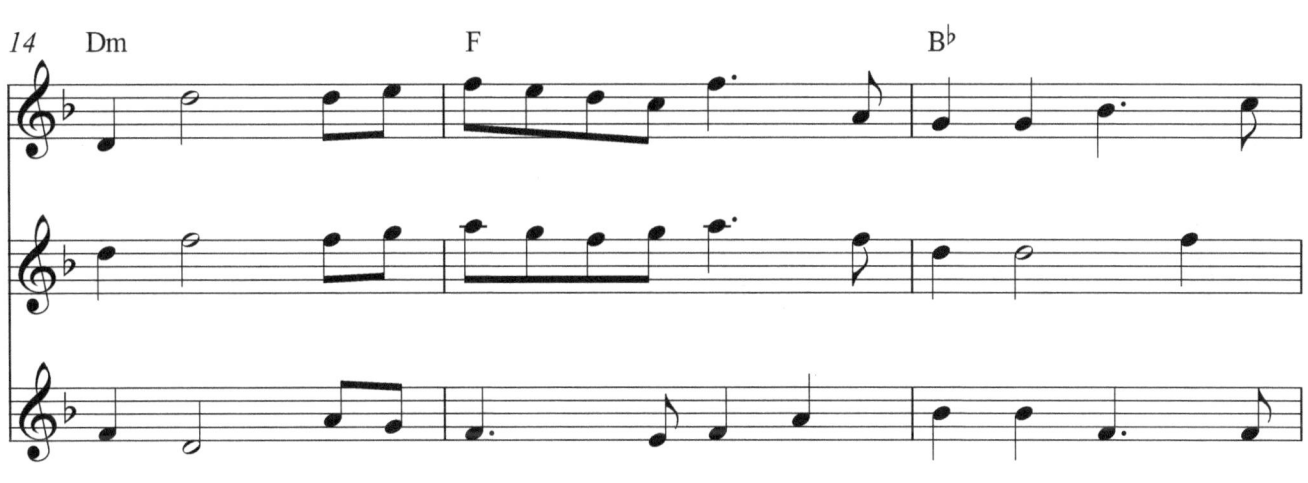

The Jolly Broom Man

Allegro ♩= 130

Trad. Morris Dance

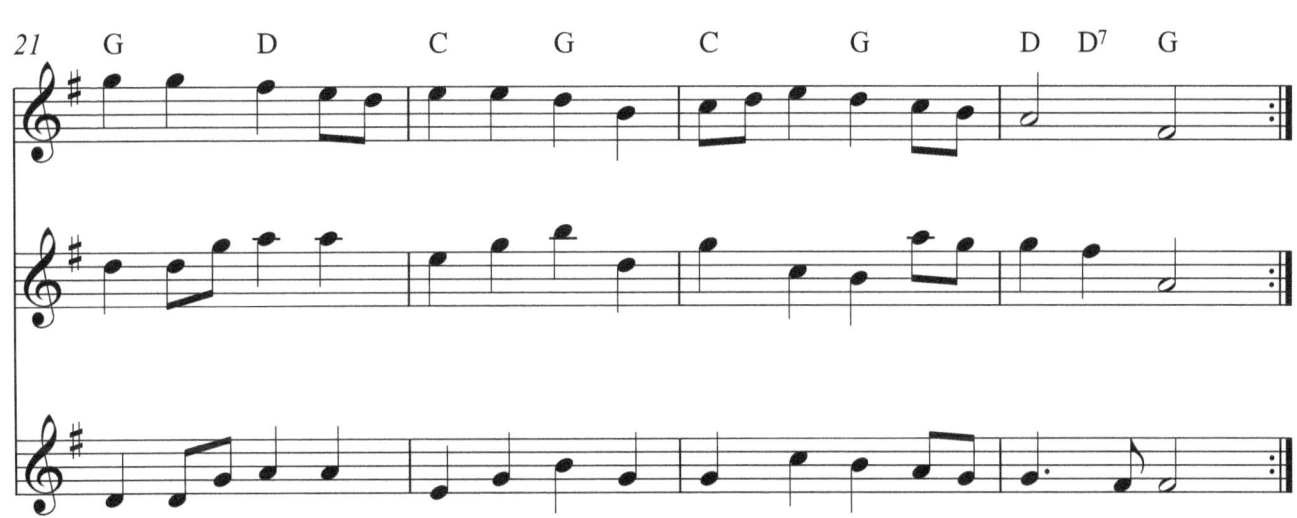

The British Grenadiers

Allegro-boldly ♩=125

Trad. Marching 18th Century

Wales

Men of Harlech – Traditional

As "The British Grenadiers" is for the England, "Men of Harlech" stands out as a rousing national song for Wales, also known as "March of the Men of Harlech." It dates back to 1794, though it relates the courage of the defenders of the seven-year siege of Harlech Castle in north Wales, from 1461–1468.

Shining Heart– Traditional

"Calon Lân" is the Welsh name for this lovely Welsh hymn. The melody and harmony date back to 1890. It has more recently been adopted by Welsh national rugby team. Thanks to a colleague, Annette Campana, who brought this to our faculty one year!

Wales

Men of Harlech

Shining Heart

Welsh Traditional

Andantino, with warmth ♩ = 90

Ireland

Down by the Sally Gardens – Traditional

The title of this song comes from a poem by W.B. Yeats. Yeats had heard an old woman singing the melody and set his famous words to it. The song is originally called "The Maids of Mourne Shore." Waldorf third-grade students know it very well as the farming song, "I Will Go with My Father a' Plowing," with words by the Irish poet, Joseph Campbell (Gaelic = *Seosamh MacCathmhaoil*). Like so many Irish airs, this has a moving and hauntingly memorable lilt.

Sí Bheag, Sí Mhór – Turlough O'Carolan

Turlough O'Carolan was a blind Irish harpist who lived in the 18th century and composed many beautiful melodies, now often played by Irish folk groups. This one, which means "the hill of the big fairies and the hill of the small fairies," is one of his best-loved and most-performed pieces.

The Star of County Down – Traditional

Another of Ireland's beautiful tunes. Found in common and in waltz time, I prefer the latter. If someone can play the penny whistle or fiddle, you can have them start with accompaniment and the ensemble join in at bar twelve.

Londonderry Air – Traditional

Often known as "Danny Boy," this is perhaps Ireland's most famous song. There are many other and perhaps better settings. I have arranged it here so at least you will have a version you can play until you find one you prefer. The melody really lends itself to a violin lead or solo until bar seventeen, when the whole ensemble can join in.

Drums and Guns – Traditional Reel

This reel is challenging but exciting to play. It is a typical Irish dance tune with repetitive figures that make your feet tap! This is a great performance piece which can include a tambour (tambourine without jingles) or shallow drum. The Irish use a hand-drum called a *bodhran* (pronounced bow-rahn), which adds very effective rhythms to dance songs.

Ireland

Down by the Sally Gardens

Si Bheag, Si Mhór

Turlough O'Carolan

Flowing ♩. = 41

Londonderry Air

Trad. Ireland

Drums and Guns

Poland

River Wisla – Traditional

One of Poland's traditional folk songs, this melody celebrates the beauty and faithfulness of the River Vistula, Poland's longest river, called *Wisla* in Poland. It also feels like a musical bridge from western to eastern European music and often melancholic mood of Russian music.

Poland

River Wisla

Andantino ♩ = 100

Trad. Poland

Russia

Little Birch Tree – Traditional

Tchaikovsky made this melody famous, but it was originally a folk melody. The birch tree is much beloved in Russia and common through all the forests and villages—and of course in many Russian fairy tales!

Troika – Traditional

The *troika* is a traditional Russian sleigh pulled by three horses. In this charming tune you can accelerate and slow down, picturing the sleigh team speeding along in the snow! It can also be used for a Russian folk dance.

Moscow Nights – Traditional

This tune, is sometimes called "Midnight in Moscow." It is should be played quite slowly. It has beautiful chord sequences and perhaps with other words could be set for a winter festival.

Christmas Candle – Traditional

This is a traditional folk tune, typically played on the balalaika. It is a lovely piece to play at Christmas, using chimes as well as recorders. It should be played quite slowly, at a tempo of about 80.

Little Birch Tree

Troika

Christmas Candle

Japan

Autumn Leaves – M. Preston

This piece tries to express the beauty and sadness of the last leaves falling in autumn. It tries to say this simply in clear, Japanese style.

Sakura – Traditional

This is a very famous song about the beautiful cherry blossoms in Japan. It should be played steadily and peacefully.

Here Is Happiness – Saburo Lida and K. Takahashi

I first heard this sweet and charming piece played on guitar for a wedding. It is a tune you can't get out of your head once you've played it a couple of times! It can be a lovely tune for graduation or some other celebration.

Japan

Autumn Leaves

Andante ♩ = 85

M. Preston

Sakura

Trad. Japan

Here Is Happiness
Koko Ni Sachi Ari

Joseph van Winkle and Fred Darian
Saburo Lida and K. Takahashi

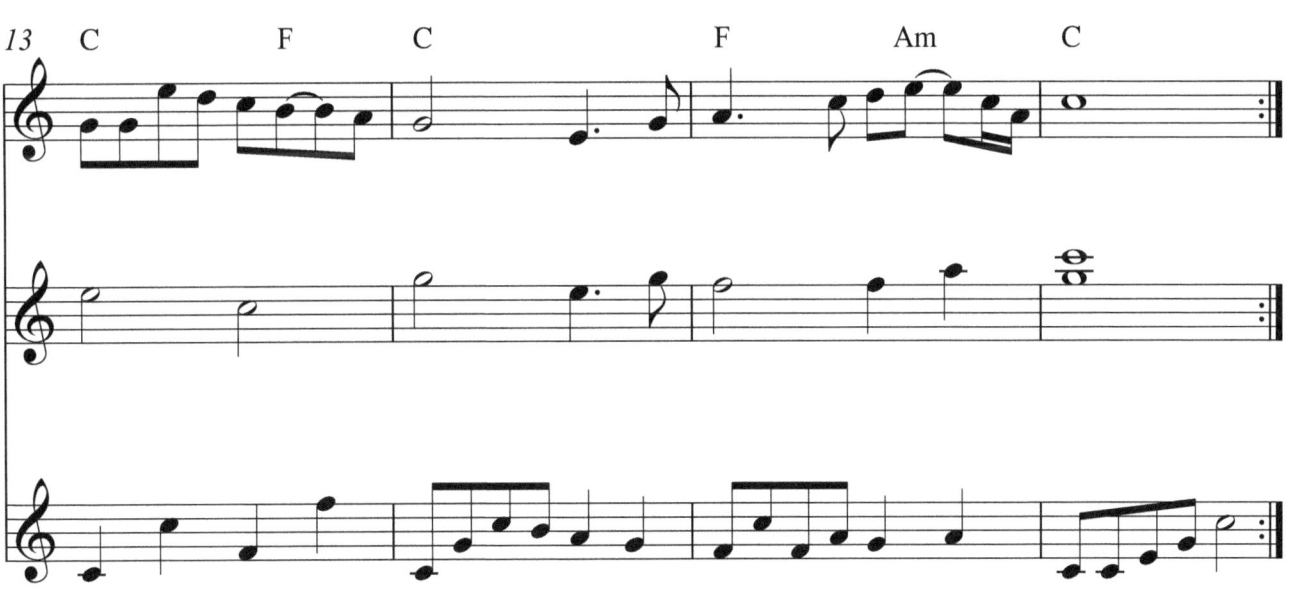

Words and Music by Saburo Lida, Kikutaro Takahashi, Joseph van Winkle and Fred Darian
Copyright © 1964 CRITERION MUSIC CORP. and SEVEN SEAS MUSIC CO. LTD. Copyright Renewed
This arrangement Copyright © 2017 CRITERION MUSIC CORP. and SEVEN SEAS MUSIC CO. LTD.
All Rights Reserved. Used by Permission. Reprinted by permission of Hal Leonard LLC

Hawai'i

Sanoe – Queen Lili'uokalani

This poignant song is about a princess and her lover, who has vanished like the mist. It was composed by the last queen of Hawai'i while she was under house arrest, after the sad overthrow of the Hawaiian kingdom. She composed many other beautiful songs.

Hawai'i Aloha – Reverend Lorenzo Lyons

This warm song has become a traditional song of unity in Hawai'i. It calls upon all to love and respect the beauty and richness of Hawai'i. The song is often sung with everyone in a circle, holding hands, at the end of community gatherings and always in Hawai'i May Day festivals.

Hawai'i

Sanoe

Andantino ♩= 100

Queen Lili'uokalani 1838-1917

Introduction

'Au — he - a 'o'e e Sa - noe _____ Ho'o - pu - lu - li - ko ka - le hu - a, E —

Hawai'i Aloha

South Pacific

Isa Lei – Fijian Anthem

This is a beautiful, heartfelt song from Fiji, though it is sung in Tonga too. It should be played slowly with warmth and dignity. There are long held notes (very typical of Polynesian music) which require a chord beat by guitar or chimes to give a steady 4/4 pulse to the tune.

Te No'o Nei Au

This song is from Raratonga, the largest of the Cook Islands, which lie between Tahiti and New Zealand. Like many songs from the South Pacific, this has a sunny and joyful rhythm! Perhaps the best version is the one sung by Robi Kahakalau from Hawai'i.

Hinanui Iti – Monique Nesa

Many Tahitian tunes have fast dance rhythms. This one is a slower, more romantic song, conjuring up a feeling of sunsets on the edge of crystal lagoons. It is common in Tahitian music to accompany the melody with a syncopated, double-speed rhythm. This gives it the special sinuosity and fire that is present in the soul of Tahiti. This rhythm comes in best at bar seventeen. You can experiment by clapping one, two-three, and syncopating and/or doubling the claps (halving the time to eighth beats). In Tahiti, the rhythm would be played on the Tahitian ukulele (often called the Tahitian banjo) which has four double strings, some pitched an octave higher than the Hawaiian ukulele.

Pokarekare Ana – P.H. Tomoana

This Maori love song from New Zealand is widely known and played and sung all over the world. It is a gentle and warm song. It can also be arranged in 4/4 time. You can hear a lovely version sung by the New Zealand singer, Hayley Westenra.

Now Is the Hour – Maori Traditional

"Now is the hour for us to say goodbye" are the opening words of this famous Polynesian farewell song. Believed to have originated in New Zealand, it is sometimes sung in Hawai'i, too. It has a flowing feeling of a canoe or ship setting out to sea. It is a very nice song to sing at the end of the school day for middle grades. (You can find additional lyrics from a variety of online sources.) It is a fitting song to end this collection of music from around the world.

South Pacific

Isa Lei

Andante moderato ♩= 100

Traditional Fijian Farewell

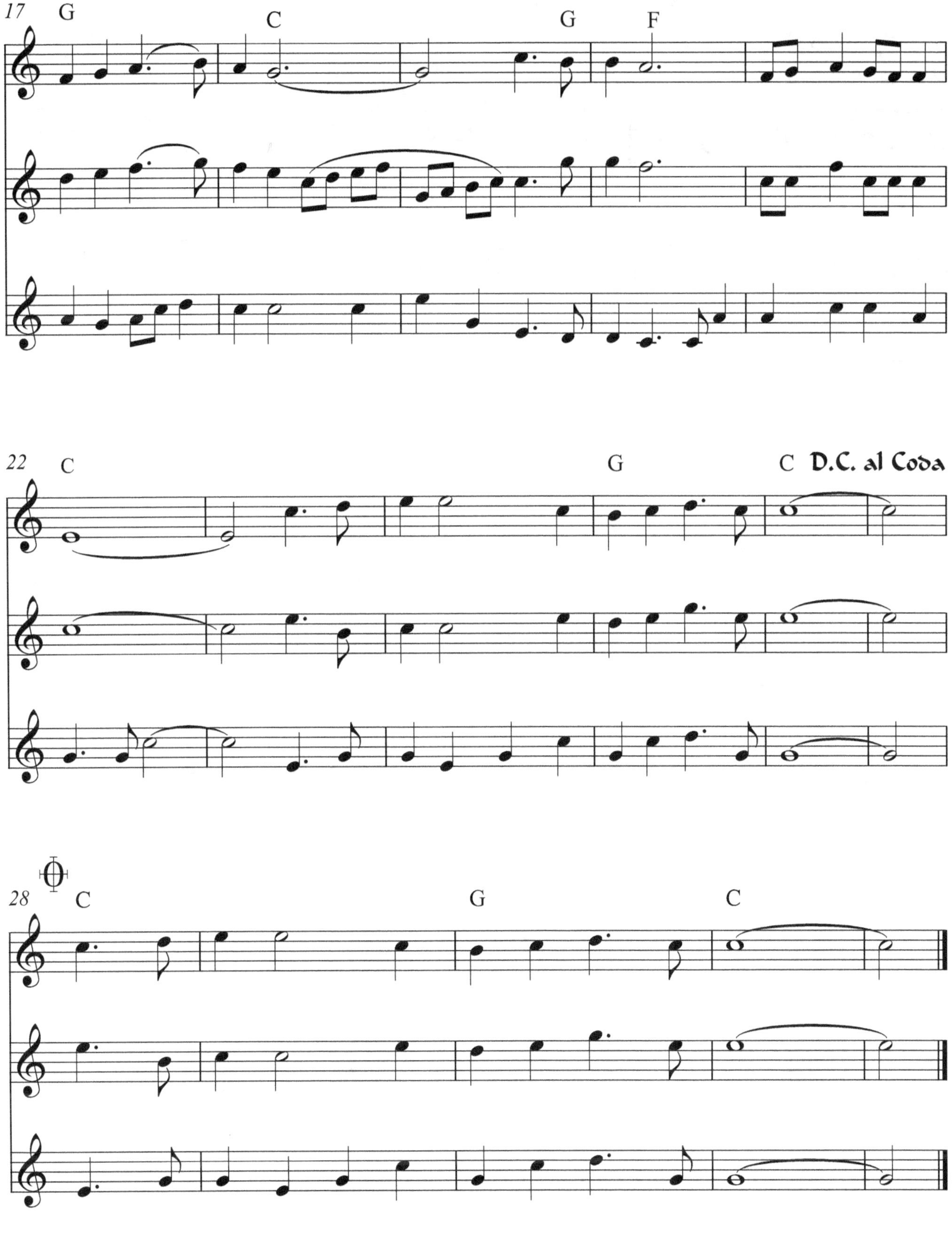
17
G
C
G
F
22
C
G
C
D.C. al Coda
28
C
G
C

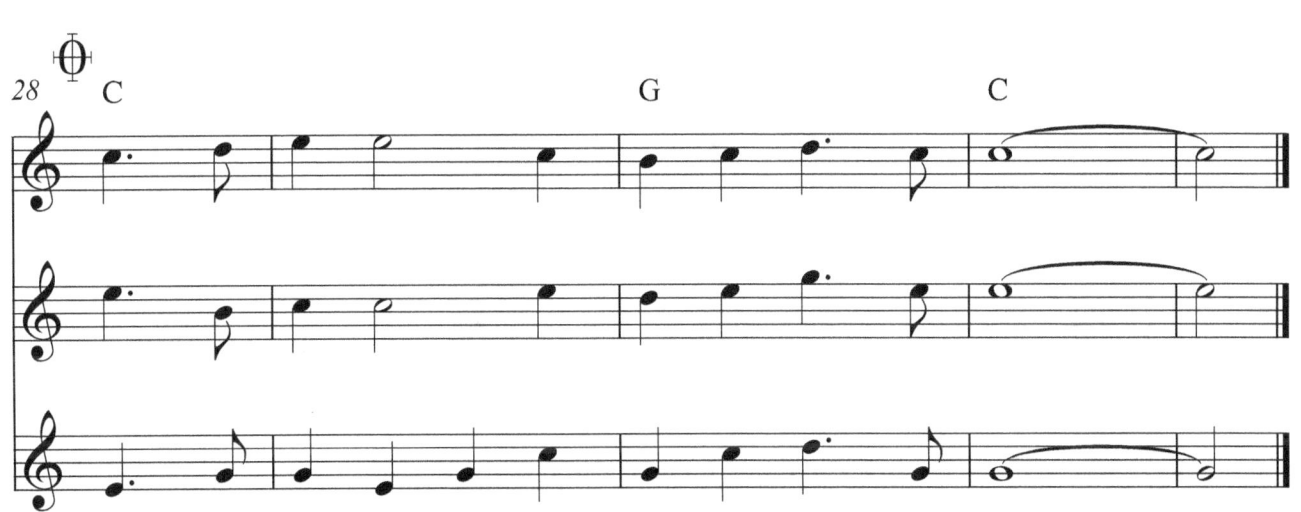

Te No'o Nei Au

Hinanui Iti

Allegro ♩ = 130

Monique Nesa

Introduction

Pokarekare Ana

Acknowledgments

Permissions

Grateful acknowledgment is given for permissions from composers and their agents to publish the recorder arrangements here, and to acquire mechanical licenses for the demonstration CD. Formal credits, where due, are given.

1. Jay Ungar and Swinging Door Music for "Ashokan Farewell" Thank you, Jay, for offering the print permission free of charge and helping me navigate the world of mechanical licenses!

2. Jim Fownes – "The Waldorf Waltz." Thank you, Jim, for your generosity in freely granting permission to include your composition and the recording in this book.

3. Kyle Cothern and GIA Publications for "Siyahamba." Thank you, Kyle, for helpful communication and granting me permission to include my recorder arrangement of this lovely piece!

4. Duron Bentley and G. Schirmer Inc. for "The Fisherman." Thank you for granting me both print and mechanical permission to include this beautiful Portuguese song in the book!

5. Shari Molstad and Hal Leonard Publishing for "Here Is Happiness." Thank you for the research and for granting print and mechanical permission to include my three-part recorder version of this charming song ("Koko Ni Sachi Ari") from Japan!

6. Raul Pileta and EGREM of Cuba for their kind permission in 2006 to include this arrangement of "Veinte Años" for three-part recorder. Their generosity in giving original permission gratis is not forgotten.

7. Tim Porter in Gloucestershire, for his two-part arrangement of "Jack's Maggot" and for musical introduction to several English and Scottish folk tunes in his folk-band collection.

Recording

Huge thanks go to Vicki Boekman of the Seattle Recorder Society for responding so enthusiastically to my search for amateur recorder players to make the CD possible. Vicki played Soprano on many tracks, as well as two of her students who joined us. She was absolutely key to organizing our meetings and recording sessions. Thank you so much, Vicki! The recordings would not have been possible without your warmth, initiative and depth of musical experience!

Isabella Pagel – Soprano. Isabella studied with Vicki since she was six years old. She has now begun her formal recorder training in Louvain, Belgium. Thank you so much for your time and skill, Isabella!

Carolyn Lober – Alto. Carolyn also studied recorder with Vicki until she graduated from high school. She began college life at Brown University fall semester 2017. Thank you, Carolyn, for your skill and all the hours you freely gave to the recording of this book!

Charles Coldwell – Tenor. A composer and recorder player, Charles played the Tenor for all of the pieces, as well as offered me invaluable advice on the scoring and musical notation of many of the pieces. Thank you, Charles, for your expertise and for the many hours you kindly gave to the recording of this book!

I am so grateful to all of you for your open-hearted generosity in freely sharing your talent and time for rehearsals and the many hours in the recording studio! The CD would not have been possible without you. Thank you all so much!

Many thanks also go out to Jack Straw Production Studio in Seattle for the use of their facilities. To Levi Fuller who seemed to effortlessly find time-slots for our recording needs—many thanks for your friendliness and efficiency!

Particular gratitude goes to Steve Ditore, our sound engineer, for his skill, patience and expert capture of the music, and his sensitive and mixing of the parts and accompaniment on guitar and ukulele. It was a pleasure to work with you, Steve. Thank you!

Illustrations

Heartfelt gratitude goes to Yukina Umezawa, who, many years after illustrating the first book when she was an 8th grader, stepped forward, in spite of her busy work schedule, to redo all the title pages for this new edition! Thank you so much, Yukina, for your patience, artistry and goodwill!

Cover

To my ever-responsive and kind son, Joseph. Thank you so much for your skill and artistry in creating such an elegant cover for this new book!

Editor

Thank you, Patrice, for your enthusiasm and ready support of this new version of the book. I am very grateful for your recognition of the importance of recorder music in schools!

Finally, I would like to honor and thank my wife, whose steady support of this project brought much sunshine to its progress. Thank you, Tanya, for your patience and goodwill!

I would again like to dedicate this book to all the hard-working teachers, wherever you may be, who love music and wish to bring it to your classes! May the tunes you choose to work on bring sparkle and much joy to your work!

www.ingramcontent.com/pod-product-compliance
Lightning Source LLC
Chambersburg PA
CBHW080437230426
43662CB00015B/2300